Poetry Treasure.

A *WordCrafter*

Poetry Anthology

Compiled and Edited by

Kaye Lynne Booth

and

Roberta Eaton Cheadle

This anthology may contain previously or simultaneously published materials.

Introduction by Kaye Lynne Booth

Compiled and edited by Kaye Lynne Booth and Roberta Eaton Cheadle.

Cover design by Teagan R. Genevieve

Notice: This anthology both American and British spellings dependant upon the country of origin of the poet.

Contents

Annette Rochelle Aben

Jude Kirya Itakali

Roberta Eaton Cheadle

In Memory of Sue Vincent

Sue Vincent was a talented poet, writer, and blogger who inspired others with her lovely images and captivating words. Her stories and poems about her four-legged friend, Ani, midnight haikus, historical and spiritual posts, and courage and determination in the face of great adversity will not be forgotten by the blogging community who loved her. Rest in peace, Sue.

Introduction

By Kaye Lynne Booth

I have always felt that poetry is very personal, more so than in other forms of writing. Poets spend endless hours placing just the right words in just the right order to say just the thing that they intend to say. Be that as it may, we still can find meaning in the poetry of others , although it may not be the same meaning the poet intended. When a poem reaches out to you, touching on experiences in your own life, that is what truly matters. That is the poet's true intent, to touch someone else with their words. It doesn't matter that it means something different to the reader than it does to the poet. What is important is that it means something, that a connection has been made.

Although not a practicing poet, I have dabbled in the art form and even have had a few published. Now days, I write mostly fiction, but poetry has always drawn me in and there has been that connection. I've offered a monthly poetry series for a couple of years now on my blog, *Writing to be Read*. The poems you find in this anthology were written by the talented poets who were guests on Robbie Cheadle's monthly blog series, "Treasuring Poetry", in 2020, and I am pleased to present them to you in this very special poetry collection.

Sue Vincent

About Sue Vincent

Sue Vincent is a Yorkshire born writer currently living in the south of England, largely due to an unfortunate incident with a map, a pin, and a blindfold. Raised in a spiritually eclectic family she has always had an unorthodox view on life, particularly the inner life, which is often reflected in her writing, poetry, and paintings.

She maintains a popular blog, *Sue Vincent's Daily Echo* at https://scvincent.com and is currently owned by Ani, the inimitable Small Dog, who also writes.

Sue lived in France for several years, sharing a Bohemian lifestyle and writing songs before returning to England where the youngest of her two sons was born. She began writing and teaching online several years ago and was invited to collaborate with Dr G. Michael Vasey on their book, "The Mystical Hexagram: The Seven Inner Stars of Power".

Since then she has published a number of books, beginning with *Swords of Destiny*, a magical tale set in the ancient landscape of Yorkshire. Her retelling of the Egyptian myths, "The Osiriad", came shortly afterwards along with her collaboration with Stuart France. Together they have written the *Triad of Albion*, the *Doomsday* trilogy and the first books in the *Lands of Exiles* series.

These books tell a true adventure in a fictional manner. They are at once a journey into the ancient and sacred landscape of Albion and the story of a growing and rather oddball friendship.

The *Triad of Albion* was followed by the *Doomsday* trilogy and the three books in the *Lands of Exile* series, where the adventures of Don and Wen stray down the paths of fiction.

They have also published a number of graphic works together exploring folklore and legend, as well as writing independently. You can read more on their blog here: https://franceandvincent.com/

Sue, along with Steve Tanham and Stuart France, is a Director of the *Silent Eye School of Consciousness*, an international modern Mystery School that seeks to allow its students to find the inherent magic in living and being. Learn more about *Silent Eye School of Consciousness* on their blog here: https://thesilenteye.co.uk/

Poetic vision

The poet sees the world through other eyes,

His vision fixed beyond horizon's span,

He walks imagination in disguise

And sees behind the humble mask of man.

Where artists fix a vision in a frame

To hold a mirror for the world to gaze,

The storyteller weaves of words a game

That leave a trail to lead them through the maze.

The poet's vision knows no earthly bound;

From high to low, wherever thought may lead,

He writes a garden where his truth is found

And from its flowers sows for us a seed.

Such bounty may be gathered from his story

To strew a path of petals home to glory.

Snowdrops

Pure

Children

Born anew

Of driven snow

Unblemished beauty

Encapsulating spring

A promise of renewal

Modest messengers of the gods

Offer hope and illumination

Shining in shadows with an inner light

Aflame

There is a hidden flame

I call it life, for want of wordless words

To compass mystery.

Burning every breath

From spark to ember days,

From ash to dust.

And whether I rise phoenix-like

Or must expire,

I choose a life aflame

Embracing fire.

Beyond the Night

Night falls;

Tenebrous swirls of amorphous shadow

Dance in the dark.

Cerements of midnight

flow and ebb

From void to oblivion

Across an empty sky.

Eyes that are raised see nothing;

Save an empty canvas... painted black;

Desire finds no shining star...

A moonless waste unbroken

By a pristine point.

Illusion reigns;

Blinding the heart,

To true perception,

Veiling with fear the inner eye

That sees beyond sight

With perfect clarity

That even in the darkest night

Beyond the horizon

The light remains.

Whispers

Stone

Silent

Unmoving

Visitors stare

Passing unaware

Of the long, slow heartbeat

The ghost of time remembers

Crystalline veins communicate

The coruscation of inner earth

The flickering flames of celebration

Honouring the origins of the stars

Reflecting ordered constellations

The ordering of the seasons

Past, present and future meld

In a time beyond time

Within hearts of stone

Wordless voices

World watchers

Whisper

Joy

Geoff Le Pard

About Geoff Le Pard

Geoff Le Pard (not Geoffrey, except to his mother) was born in 1956 and is a lawyer who saw the light. He started writing (creatively) in 2006 following a summer school course. Being a course junkie, he had spells at Birkbeck College, twice at Arvon and most recently at Sheffield Hallam where he achieved an MA in Creative Writing. And what did he learn? That they are great fun, you meet wonderful people, but the best lessons come from the unexpected places. He has a line of books some published and some still waiting. Details of his work can be found on his blog, TanGental at https://geofflepard.com/ where he writes about anything and everything. His aim is for each novel to be in a different style and genre. Most people have been nice about his writing (though when his brother's dog peed on the manuscript he was editing, he did wonder) but he knows the skill is in seeking and accepting criticism. His career in the law helped prepare him. His first book of poetry, The Sincerest Form Of Poetry was published last year.

Art Appreciation

I want to like Art collections.

I mean I love the Dutch,

Breugal and Bosch – neat little people

Intriguing encyclopaedias of paint.

And Vermeer's curious scenes,

Telling us a little, leaving us to guess.

Or Holbein's or Rembrandt's faces,

Creased, clever, detail-real people.

I can leave Reubens, frankly

With most of the Renaissance,

For a rainy day. I mean,

He's good –no doubt he can hold a brush.

And big – he really fills a canvas.

Gives good paint as they might have said.

But all those fat babies?

Today, people would wonder at his fixation.

It's when I reach that room

Floor to ceiling canvases.

Lots of clouds

And some bearded old boy who doesn't know

It's rude to point.

It's then I'm done.

My back sets like Rembrandt's granny's face.

My feet feel as if Holbein's captured their reality

And my neck is twisted into a Breugal imagined spasm.

Somewhere, in each painting, there's a little me

Suffering,

Being made an example of,

Being shown how reality really feels.

Some days I really really wish

I'd been painted by Reubens.

Ben Nevis

The summit sits alone, brooding.

It has to be aware we are coming and it can't be pleased.

We sit and fiddle with our socks

Ironing seams with our fingers

Removing granite grit

And soothing away the terror and sweaty mist to come.

The incessant ring tone of midges pricks our ears

And disturbs our skin-deep musings.

We flap a little, alert to the next pass.

On goes a shoe; we tug at laces,

Tightening the knot in our stomachs.

Still not right.

Scotland's Red Baron leads another wave,

Dive bombing our hairline,

Piercing soft exposed flesh, fracturing our temper and releasing a logarithm of pain.

We are distracted by corrugated socks, our defences are lowered

And the formation, delighted to pass through unimpeded,

Strikes the target and sucks the joy out of our walk.

The slope steepens as hopes tumble,

Horizons pile up, one on the next,

Crowding forward in their excitement.

We struggle on, the skies now clear of the air defence

But relief is as short as our breath;

Shattered lungs, gassed to shreds by effort.

And all the while the Troll in the hill slumbers;

Is he disturbed by our laboured tread?

Little irritating pinpricks distracting him from his quiet repose?

The weather is clear; squally showers pour down our faces

From the clouds in our hair, stinging our eyes with our own acid rain and drenching our vision;

Little drops of liquid midge, irritating and incessant.

We flick uselessly, trying to stem the flow.

A moment's relief and then another flood, one aggravation follows another.

The sun can't set on this Leviathan we are climbing.

We stay on his back, avoiding his gaze, sure he must be wakening to our insistent
feet.

He breathes out patches of slippery white, remnants of winter, to slow us down.

Any moment

He might rise up,

Angry,

To swat at us,

Hard.

We are so small he would miss most of us if he flapped.

We have no sharp proboscis to annoy, just our shoes, repetitive irritations

Cutting a path up his aged old back.

Would we cower and return to the fight, like midges, like sweat?

Or run like hell?

The Coffee Machine

(a homage to the office tea ladies)

Where once the cups would rattle and clink

Announcing the moment for a pause to drink

We now have freedom to hover at leisure

And choose which beverage will be our pleasure.

But the change that's reduced the trolley to scrap

And brought us instead mochas on tap

Hasn't changed the need to gather and sip,

To gossip and moan, to joke and quip.

We herd as one inside the door;

Our mugs, as Oliver's, poised for more.

Our chat, desultory, our focus keen

As we bow before the dispensing machine.

It bubbles, it fizzes, all spit and froth

Robotically delivers our chosen broth.

But I'm sad all the same as I take my fill;

Is this really better than when Emmy or Lil

Would visit each room with a twinkly grin

And knock to make sure it was right to come in.

For me, I preferred that clock-fixing cup,

When their cheery asides accompanied my sup,

And those ladies teased the nervous young man

That I was, back then, when my career began.

When I was green as the tea I drink

When I had it all to learn and time to think.

Frank Prem

About Frank Prem

Frank Prem has been a storytelling poet since his teenage years. He has been a psychiatric nurse through all of his professional career, which now exceeds forty years.

He has been published in magazines, online zines and anthologies in Australia, and in a number of other countries, and has both performed and recorded his work as spoken word.

He lives with his wife in the beautiful township of Beechworth in North East Victoria, Australia.

Frank blogs at Frank Prem Poetry which you can find here: https://frankprem.com/

Clues

there will be a clue

in violets

when the perfume rises

to force a turn to halfway

across your shoulder

searching for a source

elusive and subtle

another will gleam

inside sunlight

arrayed to warm you

with a faint suggestion

of inner glow

emerging to transpire

porous and enlightened

there will be a third

in silence

when absence is a comfort

honing the quiet senses

to enhance possibilities for receipt

of messages released

and wordlessly directed

there will be clues

for you

if you should seek them

to aid your understanding

and a clarity of mind

that reaches through dilemmas

doubts and wonder

Reading modern poets

I'm reading some modern poets

because somebody said I should

or perhaps it's more true

to say that I'm glancing at them

peering through their lives

and between their verses

I really don't care for poetry

but maybe there's an interest

in the reasons why

they wrote this line or that

(if someone's done an analysis)

or even better if they can tell me

what the writer was all about

in the middle of that night when

he or she should have been sleeping

instead of burning candles

and putting words around

a spark or a flame

before it sputtered or went out

or simply faded from mind

the way I find my thoughts do

but I really don't care for poetry

and I hope they aren't just dull and boring

people not fitted out for anything better

than a life by pen and ink

and fluffy words that try to sidestep

each obvious cliché and overworking of tired rhyme

I wonder if they read their poems in bar-rooms

to check the metre and the flow

under a half-spot light with a home-made lectern

that would make their pages fall down

all across the stage in the middle of a verse

and did they have an audience that listened

to what they said instead of only hearing

bursting Guinness bubbles or laughing out loud

at the drunk that always sits over there on poetry days

propped up in the corner and reciting Shakespeare

from the vaults of a thespian youth

and taking all my bows if there's any clapping

I'm reading some modern poets

but I really don't care for poetry

all that much

Joe Pretty-Words

there's a fella

makes his home inside the small words

of reaching and touching and dance

on the footpaths and sidewalks

of sunshine and rain

tells stories to himself

and anyone can spare a second

if they want to

to listen

if they really want to

pretty words pretty words

like christmas wrapping

and ribbons

or flowers left on a doorstep

he wants to reach out or to come inside your place

with his handful of pretty words

but who's going to listen can you tell me?

who's got the time

for touching and dancing and for reaching out?

nobody I know

no one that knows what they're doing

and anyway

what right does a joe with a pencil in his hand have

to grasp at a sky that flashes

with the twinkling of the masters

scattered across the spread of spoken words

in stanzas of movement and light?

he's only a trier coming up cheap and fast

passing from our sight like a shooting star

to burn without leaving a smoke trail

or a mark on the ether or the sky

to point out the way he went

he's just like the rest of them

so who gives a damn huh?

shhh

joe pretty-words is writing again

wonder what it is this time

anybody want to listen when he's done?

anybody?

and waits (the day; the night)

he doesn't need

help

when he rises

manages the shower

the toilet

his yellow-stained

teeth

underwear from the wire rack

drawer

coated with thick

white plastic

clean clothes

from the wardrobe

beside his bed

freshly pressed

by the laundry

takes himself

to a dayroom chair

watches through the glass . . .

the garden today

he doesn't need

any help

at mealtimes

cuts his toast

his meat

pours his own

cup of tea

no mess

on his clothing

no stains

no food debris

on the floor

no need

to speak

at all

and

he's not really one

for the entertainments

no

so he doesn't attend the

crucifix-on-a-table

that serves the mass

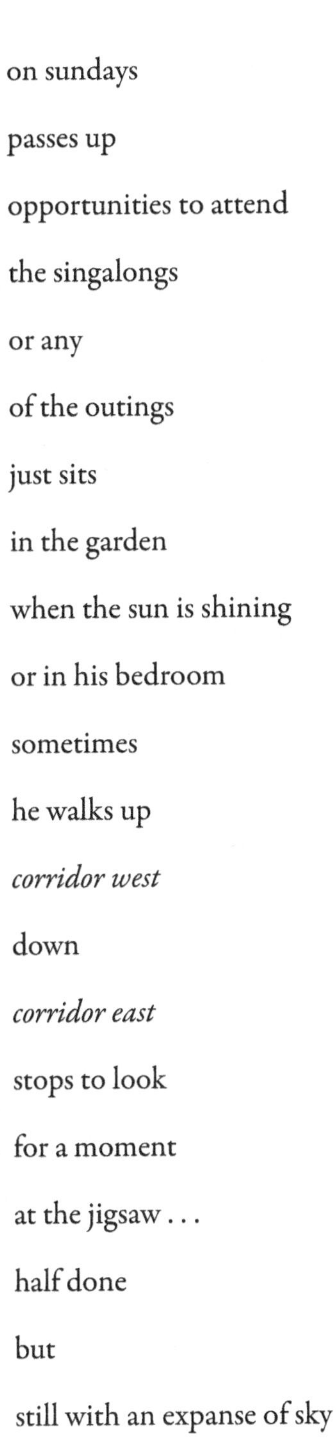

on sundays

passes up

opportunities to attend

the singalongs

or any

of the outings

just sits

in the garden

when the sun is shining

or in his bedroom

sometimes

he walks up

corridor west

down

corridor east

stops to look

for a moment

at the jigsaw . . .

half done

but

still with an expanse of sky

lying in jumbled pieces

on a table

in the alcove

at corridor end

and he doesn't need

help

in the evening

at all

puts himself to bed

early

takes no tablets

says a quiet

good night nurse

and lets her

turn the light out

watches raindrops grow

heavy

then trickle

down the glass pane

of his window

and waits

for sleep

the slow world (of the juggler)

he had riffled

through maintenance

and through stores

three wrenches

two shrink-wrapped trays

of ration packs

~

the boredom

of a day

that is only

a day

because the lights

are turned on

of performing

a maintenance function

when no maintenance

is needed

these

are long

l

o

n

g

hours

~

he threw

a heavy wrench -

red -

into the air

a box

of breakfast

the silver spanner

one of lunch

the bolt tightener

~

a graceful

arc

of objects thrown

the slight gravity

of his work-out room

allowing gentle descent

of each

thrown object

up . . .

slowly

down . . .

up . . .

he has time

to see

and to adjust

positions himself

to catch

and to recast

each tool

and all rations

just so

varying the height

of his peaks

according to whim

and

increasing skill

~

daytime

defined by the

luminescence

of selected

internal light

can be a long

tedious

affair

Victoria (Tori) Zigler

About Victoria Zigler

Victoria Zigler is a blind vegan poet and children's author. Born and raised in the shadow of the Black Mountains of Wales, UK, she moved away from Wales three times: once to spend six months living in Alberta, Canada, the other times to spend a few years living near Hastings on the South-East coast of England, UK, each time returning to Wales. Now she lives in Wales again, along with a chinchilla named Mollie, a West Highland White Terrier named Lilie, a Cavapoo named Logan, a Hermann's Tortoise named Artemis, and her Canadian husband, Kelly.

Despite spending far more time than she'd have liked in hospital, and eventually losing her sight to Congenital Glaucoma, Victoria - or Tori, if you prefer - has been writing since she knew how, with no plans to stop any time soon. So far, she has published nine poetry books and 46 children's books, all of which are available from a variety of online retailers in multiple eBook formats, as well as in both paperback and audio. She's also contributed a story to the sci-fi and fantasy anthology *Wyrd Worlds II*, which is available in eBook only. Additionally, Tori's Hermann's tortoise, Artemis, was featured in both the *Magnificent Pets Coloring*

Book For Children and the *Magnificent Pets Mandala Coloring Book For Adults*, which are available via *Praise My Pet*.

Vegan due to both a love for animals and diatary allergy, as well as an Eclectic Pagan, Tori describes herself as a combination of Hermione Granger and Luna Lovegood from the *Harry Potter* books: Hermione's thirst for knowledge and love of books, combined with Luna's wandering mind and alternative way of looking at the world. She has a wide variety of interests, designed to exercise both the creative and logical sides of her brain, and dabbles in them at random depending on what she feels like doing at any given time, but is most likely to be found playing with her pet-kids, curled up somewhere with a cup of tea and a book, or trying to keep one step ahead of those pesky typo fairies while writing her own books.

Victoria blogs at Zigler News here: https://ziglernews.blogspot.com/

The Robin In My Garden

The robin in my garden

Sings his joyful tune

Of hope for the future

And Spring arriving soon

And when his song is over

He'll go on his merry way

Little knowing just how much

He brightened up my day

Hello Insomnia, My Old Friend

Near a mountain covered in sheep

I toss and turn, but fail to sleep.

In despair I'm almost weeping

For I wish that I was sleeping.

But as I lay here in my bed

Thoughts are buzzing in my head,

And that's why I'm already dreading

The direction this night is heading.

Hello insomnia, my old friend,

Our relationship has got to end.

A Grain of Sand

A grain of sand may not look like much;

So tiny it evades your touch.

But a grain of sand has something to teach,

As it joins with others to form a beach.

Just think of all the things we could do,

If we worked together like grains of sand do.

Colleen M. Chesebro

About Colleen M. Chesebro

Colleen M. Chesebro is a Michigan Poet who loves crafting syllabic poetry, flash fiction, and creative fiction and nonfiction. Colleen sponsors a weekly syllabic poetry challenge, called *Tanka Tuesday*, on wordcraftpoetry.com where participants learn how to write traditional and current forms of haiku, senryu, haiga, tanka, gogyohka, tanka prose, renga, solo-renga, haibun, cinquain, Etheree, nonet, shadorma, Badger's hexastich, Abhanga, and diatelle poetry.

Colleen's syllabic poetry has appeared in the *Auroras & Blossoms Poetry Journal*, and in "*Hedgerow, a journal of small poems*," and in various other online publications. She's won many awards from participating in the *Carrot Ranch Rodeo*, a yearly 99-word flash fiction contest sponsored by carrotranch.com, an online writing community. Recently, she created the Double Ennead, a 99-syllable poetry form for Carrot Ranch.

Colleen has published a collection of poetry, flash fiction, and short stories called "*Fairies, Myths & Magic: A Summer Celebration*," dedicated to the Summer Solstice. She contributed a short story called "*The Changeling*," in the "*Ghostly Rites Anthology 2020*" published by *Plaisted Publishing House*.

Colleen Chesebro's poetry blog is called Word Craft – Prose & Poetry at https://wordcraftpoetry.com/

Her author blog is found at https://colleenchesebro.com where you will find her poetry and short stories.

The Weather Witch

Double Inverted Nonet

My guiding light was a weather witch.

She taught me to mix the winds and

to call down the lightening.

yet, I've seen her in rain

not utter a spell.

Her power was

natural –

bound by

trust

in

magic

and with the

understanding

that choice designed with

the use of elements

held no power over them.

Her strength lay with separating

The light from the darkness held within.

The Connection

Haibun Senryu

My walk resulted in a surprise this morning. I found a toadstool growing on the north side of a Palo Verde tree where the sprinkler had sprung a leak. It's unusual to see a toadstool in the desert, so I suspected there was magic afoot.

The late summer sun hung in the early sky; an angry red orb smothered by wildfire smoke. Cool air currents swirled around my legs, mixing with the warmer currents above. I followed the winding path along the wall that edged the sprawling desert surrounding my housing area, listening to the sounds of the birds in the trees.

Ahead, a woman and her dog, dawdled. She'd tug his leash to suggest a turn in the path, but he'd have nothing to do with any changes in his plans. He planted his feet, refusing to budge, and watched my steady approach.

I remembered this dog from another walk. He's an older gent with only one eye; maybe a terrier mix. Like me, his hair has turned silver and grey.

When I finally caught up to him, the dog wriggled across the path, wagging a stub of a tail in greeting.

"Hello, Sir Galahad," I called out. I didn't know his actual name, but this name seemed to fit. I held out my hand, and he gave it a quick lick. I scratched his head, and he shivered in delight. Both of us connected for that second, bonded in the simple pleasure of connecting with another like soul.

"He waited for you," his owner said. "He wouldn't take the turn until he could see you."

I nodded my head. "I noticed he waited for me."

The lady smiled back as Sir Galahad scampered to her side. "He definitely has his favorites."

"You know what?" I called over to her. "That little guy just made my day."

"That's his specialty," she answered, with a knowing look on her face.

The two of them turned down the fork in the path, and I realized how important this connection felt to me. I turned toward home, and noticed my steps were lighter, as if someone had lifted some tremendous weight, I hadn't known I carried around my shoulders.

look for the magic

In everyday occurrences

Friendship feeds your soul

The Sun, Moon & Stars

Double Ennead created by Colleen Chesebro: 3 stanzas of (6/5/11/6/5) 99-syllable poetry

winter, under sun's glow

snow-light reflections

fluoresce, blinding our senses to the cold –

days when the algid winds

toss thoughts like snowflakes

winter, under moon's glow

purple shadows float

reflecting the darkness before dawn's ascent –

tiny souls sleepy-eyed

dreaming of the spring

winter, under star's glow

snow crystals glisten

expecting the thaw and the warm rains to come –

sun, moon, and stars carry

the hope of new life

K. Morris

About K. Morris

Kevin Morris was born in Liverpool, on 6 January 1969. He attended the Royal School for the Blind and Saint Vincent's School for the Blind (both of which are located in Liverpool). He has happy memories of leafing through "Palgrave's Golden Treasury", "The Oxford Book of English Verse" and other poetry collections in the school library. It was during his time in the school library, together with the many hours spent sitting on his grandfather's knee as he read to him, that Kevin derived his love of literature and poetry in particular.

Kevin read history and politics at University College Swansea and graduated with a BA (joint hons) and a MA in political theory.

In 1994 Kevin moved to London where he now lives and works. He is lucky to live close to an historic park in the Upper Norwood/Crystal Palace area (a suburb of greater London). Upper Norwood derives its name from the Great North Wood and is one of the greenest parts of greater London.

Kevin uses a standard Windows computer equipped with software called Job Access with Speech or JAWS, which converts text into speech and braille enabling him to compose his poetry and perform other tasks on his computer.

You will find some of Kevin's poetry on his lovely blog here: https://kmorrispoet.com/

<u>The five poems presented in this anthology first appeared in *The Further Selected Poems of K Morris* published on Amazon on 27 February 2021 in Kindle and paperback.</u>

Whilst Drunk on Very Strong Beer

Whilst drunk on very strong beer

I met the late Edward Lear.

When I said, "you are dead!",

He turned to me and said,

"Yes, but I fancied a beer!"

Miss Shakespeare

I know a barmaid called Miss Shakespeare

Who has pulled me many a beer.

The old barman, named Macbeth,

Bores us all to death.

And King Duncan is off his beer.

Whilst visiting The Great Count Dracula

Whilst visiting the great Count Dracula

I said, "your view is truly spectacular.

But your breath is quite foul,

And those wolves they do howl!

I regret I must leave Castle Dracula!"

I Hear The Rain

I hear the rain, again.

How it does pour,

Over city street, and moor

When I go my way,

The rain will stay.

And others will remain,

Listening to the rain.

Lonely Train

I have no resistance

To the lonely train

Which calls

From the distance.

Nor to the rain

Which falls,

In this dark park.

Annette Rochelle Aben

About Annette Rochelle Aben

I was born writing! At least this is how it seems. I had the good fortune to be published while a sophomore in high school, so continuing the journey by publishing books has been a natural course of events.

It is my pleasure to announce that the book I have just released is # 1 Best Seller! And that is: *A Haiku Perspective 2018*, which is available in both Kindle and paperback formats! Enjoy celebrating a year of my life as told using the framework of Haiku style poetry.

Angel Messages Two - songs of the heart, is a book filled with beautiful photos and remarkable tanka poetry. People LOVE this book because of the comfort it provides. Many have gifted it to others and been thanked over and over again.

A Tanka Picture Book is exactly as the name suggests. I took photos of a variety of everyday objects, works of art and nature, then wrote a tanka poem for each. I suggest this book for all the right reasons. It will entertain, provoke thought, stimulate conversation and be a great addition to your library!

I have chosen to release my annual haiku collection in time to celebrate National Poetry Month, in April. *A Haiku Perspective 2017* is filled with smiles, laughter, wisdom and creativity, all cleverly disguised as haiku poetry. Enjoy!

My book, *GO YOU* offers some encouragement when you need it. It is a pep-talk in a book! Each page gives you a quick way to start your day, help you through a moment or even provide someone else words that can inspire them to a better life. We can all use a cheerleader, when one isn't available, this book fits the bill!

Most of the books I have published here are centered in poetry, Haiku poetry to be exact. Much of the feedback I receive about the haiku poetry is that people can really understand the messages and they appreciate that the poems are short and sweet!

Angel Messages - a wing and a prayer is my first book about angels. Filled with photos, prayers, poems and prose of and about Angels, this book will delight any Angel lover in your life. Check out the reviews, people are drawn to the inherent inspirational nature of this book and as result is fast becoming their favorite. You can have it right away using the Kindle option or order a paperback copy (or two) and carry it with you wherever you go.

I mentioned that many of my books are filled with my poetry and several of them combine that with my love of taking pictures. Books that feature poetry and photos include *Perspective*, it's all about replacing one thought with another, *PhoKu*, visual perspective haiku and *BooKu*, Halloween haiku. *Perspective* has a wide variety of pages that feature prose, poetry and nature photographs, while *PhoKu* is filled with the photographs I have taken in nature with Haiku poetry added to them, hence the title: *PhoKu*. *BooKu* is a "behind the scenes look at how Halloween decorations feel about their jobs. All three of these books are available in print and Kindle formats.

A Haiku Perspective 2015, and *A Haiku Perspective 2016* are haiku poetry books. When I first experimented with the haiku writing format, I had no idea I would enjoy it as much as I do. These days, I am writing haiku daily and finding myself thinking in 17 syllables. You can find these books in both print and Kindle formats.

Annette Rochelle Aben has a blog of the same name here: https://annetterochelleaben.wordpress.com/

Room to Grow

A tanka

We recycle here

Plastic, paper, cans of tin

Can all find new life

Giving us a cleaner world

Reducing the heaps and mounds

Thank YOU

A senryu

Since you dare to dream

Tomorrow belongs to you

You've created it

Yes

A tanka

Love is for giving

And forgiving is to love

When we are loving

Forgiving isn't needed

For we're loving what we give

Jude Kirya Itakali

About Jude Kirya Itakali

Deep down, I think I have always known writing was a part of me. The way I would swoon at a lovely bit of prose, even when I did not know it was prose. The way I would review each book, even as a little boy.

But mostly, I knew because each time I read something, I longed to share my thoughts; to imagine and create a new perspective, to pull out this, and borrow that. And thus, to write a story of my own.

I find a good narrative, and poetry (in-every-which-way), impossible to resist.

I'm an African writer who has been raised in a global world. Half the lore and traditions I know are not my own, and yet feel like a part of me.

I love to connect with writers and those in love with literature, to share, and mostly to learn.

Fantasy and fiction are wonderful escapes for me.

Writing and reading takes me to places I have not yet been and has brought me a freedom that previously evaded me.

I appreciate great photography and totally believe in empathy. I think that every story has an impact, especially when told in a right way, and that's one thing I enjoy doing; telling these tales.

You can find most of my poetry and prose, fiction and creative writing on my blog 'tales told different' here: https://wordeologist.wordpress.com/

Darkness and Light

Darkness leave me be

This misery needs no company

So why does my broken heart

Break all in its path

Why do I love and despise love

Like the dead despise the living

And yet still long to join them

I have sought the light

But it's blinding to my eyes

I have struck the match

But the fire burns me dry

What love do I need

And what love can I give

I beseech the heavens

For just one lonely star

In this vast bleak darkness

I seek an ember of hope

To spark my dying Will

And ignite my failing spirit

For in each and every darkness

There is light, eager to shine.

Self-Love

This lonely soul of mine

Dwells in an endless winter

Disguising need in jibes and jests

Camouflaging desire in lies and aspersions

And sieving love through reason

My heart longs for one who'll break its barriers

One who will lay nude its insecurities

Reach for the longing deep inside

And the beauty woven, in every soul

I seek another

But the answer lies within

For the key to my soul's freedom

Has always been with me

The care of the body

The nurture of the mind

And the pursuit of dreams

As I learn to love, these aspects of my being

I take the first step

On the path to happiness

Soulmate

She rides the winds of change

Cool of touch

But warming of heart

Cajoling despair

Soothing distress

And whispering with a fragrance of bright futures

She whisks the dread of fate away

Its jealous shadow

That looms over happiness

Its spiteful gaze

That stalks behind lovers

All its gloom and doom,

Has fled before her healing onslaught

She has drizzled the rains of hope

And glimmered the light of rebirth

Sharing in my dreams

And lacing them with hers

She thaws the winter in my soul

And spring now blossoms within

For she loved me into loving again

And my heart has been hers since then

Roberta Eaton Cheadle

About Roberta Eaton Cheadle

I am a South African writer specialising in historical, paranormal and horror novels and short stories. I am an avid reader in these genres and my writing has been influenced by famous authors including Bram Stoker, the Bronte sisters, Amor Towles, Stephen Crane, Enrich Maria Remarque, George Orwell, Stephen King, and Colleen McCullough.

I was educated at the University of South Africa where I achieved a Bachelor of Accounting Science in 1996 and a Honours Bachelor of Accounting Science in 1997. I was admitted as a member of The South African Institute of Chartered Accountants in 2000.

I have worked in corporate finance from 2001 until the present date and have written seven publications relating to investing in Africa. I have won several awards over my twenty-year career in the category of Transactional Support Services.

I have been published a number of anthologies and have two published YA books, *While the Bombs Fell* and *Through the Nethergate*. I have recently published my first adult novel called *A Ghost and His Gold* which is partly set in South Africa during the Second Anglo Boer War.

Roberta Eaton Cheadle blogs at *Roberta Writes* here: https://robertawrites235681907.wordpress.com/ and *Robbie's Inspiration* here: https://robbiesinspiration.wordpress.com/blog/

What is happiness?

What is happiness?

Can it ever be found

by a turbulent spirit

in perpetual motion?

Eyes that see too much

Ears that hear too much

Nerves that sense too much

A heart that feels too much

Is happiness the tranquillity

of a mind at rest?

Undisturbed by the debris

of our media destruction

societal polarization

religious fragmentation and

corporate domination

Is happiness tangible

like a wallet full of money?

Could I catch it in my hands

like a ball round and smooth?

Or will it run through my fingers

like a wave on the shore?

Is intellectual prowess

and the mind that probes

the antithesis of that favoured state

called happiness?

Could someone help, please,

and give me some clarity?

How I see

How I see

and how you see

will differ

How much we differ

will depend

on how you view

what we both see

versus how I view

what we both see

That same scene

could be interpreted

by you

in a most literal

and straight forward way

You could take the path

well-worn by the majority

and embrace it

as your own

I, on the other hand,

may chose to take

a unique approach

demarcated by difference

the one chosen by few

or even none other at all

Where you see mild damage

I may see calamity

Where you see death

I may see a new beginning

Where you see straight lines

I may see soft curves

of great hope

Does this make me wrong

and you right?

If I stand alone

and you concur with many?

Or is there still room

For differing interpretations?

Tears

Collecting in pools

A nation's gushing tears

As people lose hope

The I

There comes a time

when thoughts of they

transform into the I

It's even worse

when the idea of we

becomes a solitary me

When does this occur?

I hear you ask

With curiosity and doubt

when could this possibly be?

When could the generosity

in each man's heart

turn to such selfish thoughts as these

I think it's when,

my astounded friends,

survival raises its ugly head

Acts of care and kindness

when I is sufficiently threatened

are sure to freeze inside the veins

and compassion, I'm afraid

no longer flows freely

when it comes to a difficult choice

"What about my kids?" I will surely say

"I've worked hard for what I've got

Struggled to be the one

to go the extra mile

and I'll not give it up

to improve the lot of those others."

Don't you know, dear friend?

Can you really not see,

that this I of which we speak

is spelled with a capital letter

I know you must recognise

that I must come first

it's the natural order of events

after all, is the saying not

I'm okay Jack, which surely means

I'm first in line to keep my share

when the goodies start running short.

There was a young woman

Covid-19 twisted nursery rhyme

> There was a young woman
>
> who lived in a shoe
>
> When coronavirus hit
>
> it caused quite a set-to
>
> She gave the children a laptop
>
> with matching headphones
>
> and forced them to home school
>
> ignoring their moans and groans.

Thank You for Reading

Poetry Treasures.

If you Enjoyed this anthology, be sure to leave a review and support the author/Poets found within.

I hope you have enjoyed ***Poetry Treasures***. Drop by *Writing to be Read*, the place where this anthology began, to find more "Treasuring Poetry" author/poet interviews and reviews by Robbie Cheadle, as well as other valuable content from Robbie, Jeff Bowles, Arthur Rosch and Kaye Lynne Booth.

If you follow the blog and let me know in an email at KLBWordCrafter@gmail.com, I will send you a free copy of the writer's reference, ***Ask the Authors***, which also originated from a blog series on *Writing to be Read* and was published by *WordCrafter Press*.

About the Publisher

WordCrafter Press publishes quality books and anthologies. Learn more about *WordCrafter* and keep updated on current online book events, writing contests, up coming book blog tours and new releases on the *Writing to be Read* authors' blog: https://writingtoberead.com/